AND FUN ABOUT THE PRESIDENTS

GEORGE SULLIVAN

Illustrated by Robert Roper

SCHOLASTIC INC.
New York Toronto London Auckland Sydney

ISBN 0-590-44428-X

Copyright © 1987 by George Sullivan.
All rights reserved. Published by Scholastic Inc.

12 11 10 9 8 7   2 3 4 5/9

Printed in the U.S.A.   01

First Scholastic printing, January 1987

HELP WANTED

Four-year position available with 200-year-old firm. Possible opportunity for renewal. Applicant must be over 35 years of age, have lived in the U.S. for at least 14 years. Only natural-born citizens will be considered. Salary: $200,000. Housing and meals included, also use of weekend and vacation retreat. Free travel, own police force, domestic servants, other fringe benefits. Excellent retirement plan. Good opportunity for the right person.

☆ Payday ☆

The President receives a salary of $200,000 a year. While that may seem like a great deal of money, bear in mind that it is only about half the amount earned by the average major league baseball player. And the President doesn't get the winters off.

The President is also provided with a $50,000-a-year expense account and a $40,000 allowance for travel and entertainment.

These amounts are established by Congress. The President's salary has increased dramatically as the duties and responsibilities of the office have grown. Another factor, of course, has been the rise in the cost of living.

Here is a breakdown of Presidential salaries from the time of George Washington.

$25,000 Salary

George Washington
John Adams
Thomas Jefferson
James Madison
James Monroe
John Quincy Adams
Andrew Jackson
Martin Van Buren
William H. Harrison

John Tyler
James K. Polk
Zachary Taylor
Millard Fillmore
Franklin Pierce
James Buchanan
Abraham Lincoln
Andrew Johnson
Ulysses S. Grant
  (first term)

$50,000 Salary

Ulysses S. Grant
  (second term)
Rutherford B. Hayes
James A. Garfield
Chester A. Arthur

Benjamin Harrison
Grover Cleveland
William McKinley
Theodore Roosevelt

$75,000 Salary plus $25,000 Travel Allowance

William H. Taft
Woodrow Wilson
Warren G. Harding

Calvin Coolidge
Herbert C. Hoover
Franklin D. Roosevelt

$100,000 Salary plus $40,000 Travel and Entertainment Allowance and $50,000 Expense Account

Harry S. Truman

John F. Kennedy

Dwight D. Eisenhower

Lyndon B. Johnson

$200,000 Salary plus $40,000 Travel and Entertainment Allowance and $50,000 Expense Account

Richard M. Nixon

James E. Carter

Gerald R. Ford

Ronald W. Reagan

☆ Next in Line ☆

If the President dies, resigns, or is removed from office, the Vice President takes over. Next in line after the Vice President, according to legislation passed by Congress in 1947 and in 1955, are the following government officials:

1. Speaker of the House
2. President *Pro Tempore* of the Senate
3. Secretary of State
4. Secretary of the Treasury
5. Secretary of Defense
6. Attorney General
7. Secretary of the Interior

8. Secretary of Agriculture
9. Secretary of Commerce
10. Secretary of Labor
11. Secretary of Health and Human Services
12. Secretary of Housing and Urban Development
13. Secretary of Transportation
14. Secretary of Energy
15. Secretary of Education

☆ The Long and the Short of It ☆

At 6 feet, 4 inches, Abraham Lincoln was the tallest of the Presidents. The shortest, James Madison, stood 5 feet, 4 inches. Here's a Presidential ranking by height.

Abraham Lincoln	6 feet, 4 inches
Lyndon B. Johnson	6 feet, 3 inches
Thomas Jefferson	6 feet, 2½ inches
Franklin D Roosevelt	6 feet, 2 inches
George Washington	6 feet, 2 inches
Chester Alan Arthur	6 feet, 2 inches
Ronald Reagan	6 feet, 1 inch
Andrew Jackson	6 feet, 1 inch
James Monroe	6 feet
Gerald Ford	6 feet

John F. Kennedy	6 feet
John Tyler	6 feet
James Buchanan	6 feet
William H. Taft	6 feet
James Garfield	6 feet
Warren G. Harding	6 feet
Richard Nixon	5 feet, 11½ inches
Herbert Hoover	5 feet, 11 inches
Woodrow Wilson	5 feet, 11 inches
Grover Cleveland	5 feet, 11 inches
Dwight D. Eisenhower	5 feet, 10½ inches
Calvin Coolidge	5 feet, 10 inches
Franklin Pierce	5 feet, 10 inches
Andrew Johnson	5 feet, 10 inches

Theodore Roosevelt	5 feet, 10 inches
Jimmy Carter	5 feet, 9½ inches
Harry Truman	5 feet, 9 inches
Millard Fillmore	5 feet, 9 inches
Rutherford B. Hayes	5 feet, 8½ inches
Ulysses S. Grant	5 feet, 8½ inches
William H. Harrison	5 feet, 8 inches
James K. Polk	5 feet, 8 inches
Zachary Taylor	5 feet, 8 inches
William McKinley	5 feet, 7 inches
John Adams	5 feet, 7 inches
John Quincy Adams	5 feet, 7 inches
Martin Van Buren	5 feet, 6 inches
Benjamin Harrison	5 feet, 6 inches
James Madison	5 feet, 4 inches

☆ President for a Day ☆

David Rice Atchison. Few people know the name. Yet some claim that David Rice Atchison was a President of the United States, and that history books should recognize him as such.

The claim is made on the basis of this evidence:

Zachary Taylor won the presidential election of 1848. The four-year term of the outgoing President, James K. Polk, and his Vice President, George Mifflin Dallas (for whom the city of Dallas, Texas, is named), was to end at noon on March 4, 1849. Zachary Taylor was scheduled to take the presidential oath of office that same day.

But Taylor decided that he didn't want to take the oath of office on March 4 because it was a Sunday. He announced he would wait until the next day, Monday, March 5.

That meant that from noon on March 4, 1849, when Polk's term expired, until noon of March 5, when Taylor would be sworn in, there would be no elected President or Vice President in office.

A law had been enacted by Congress on March 1, 1792, that provided that "in case of the removal, death, resignation or disability of both the President and Vice President of the United States, the President of the Senate *Pro Tempore* shall act as President." (The Vice President presides over the Senate. The Senate selects a President *Pro Tempore*, a temporary President, who presides during the absence of the Vice President.)

The President of the Senate *Pro Tem-*

pore at the time that Polk's term of office came to an end was David Rice Atchison. He served from noon on March 4, 1849, until Zachary Taylor took the oath of office at noon on March 5. David Rice Atchison was President for a day.

Although Atchison was never actually sworn in as President, never signed any legislation and never lived in the White House, some people think that he deserves to be listed with Washington, Jefferson; Lincoln, Kennedy, Reagan and all the others.

Atchison died in 1886. The state of Missouri erected a monument in his honor. It bears this inscription: "David Rice Atchison. President of the U.S. for one day. Lawyer, statesman and jurist."

☆ The First Time ☆

- George Washington was the first President whose likeness appeared on a U.S. postage stamp. The stamp was issued in 1847.

- John Adams, who followed Washington in office, was the first President to live in the White House.

Adams and his wife moved in°on November 1, 1800. (The White House was under construction during Washington's administration.)

- Thomas Jefferson was the first President to be inaugurated in Washington, D.C. The date was March 4, 1801. John Adams, who preceded Jefferson, took the oath of office in Philadelphia. George Washington, Adams's predecessor, was inaugurated in New York for his first term, and Philadelphia for his second.

- The first President to ride on a steamship was James Monroe. The vessel was the *Savannah*; the date was 1819.

- Andrew Jackson, born on March 15, 1767, was the first President to be born in a log cabin.

- Martin Van Buren, born on December 5, 1782, was the first President to be born a citizen of the United States. Previous Presidents had been born before the American Revolution, and thus were born British subjects.

- At a White House reception on July 4, 1801, Jefferson introduced the custom of having male guests shake hands. In previous administrations, men had bowed stiffly.

- James Madison, who served from 1809–1817, was the first President to wear regularly long trousers instead of knee breeches.

- William Henry Harrison, the ninth President, was the first to die in office. When he died (on April 4, 1841), he had been President for only 32 days.

- John Tyler was the first President to marry while in office. On June 26, 1844, Tyler married Julia Gardner in New York City.

- Abraham Lincoln was the first President to be born outside the borders of the thirteen original states. Lincoln was born in Hodgenville, Hardin County, Kentucky, on February 12, 1809.

- The first President to visit the West Coast was Rutherford B. Hayes. He arrived in San Francisco during September 1880.

- In 1909, William Howard Taft, the twenty-seventh President, was the first to have an automobile at the White House.

- The first American President to visit a foreign country was Woodrow Wilson. He sailed for France, on December 4, 1918, to negotiate the peace treaty ending World War I.

- Herbert Hoover, born in West Branch, Iowa, on August 10, 1874, was the first President born West of the Mississippi River.

- Hoover was also the first President to have a telephone in his office. It was installed on his desk in 1929. Before that, the White House telephone had been located in a booth outside the Executive Office.

- Franklin D. Roosevelt was the first President elected to a third term (in 1940). He was also elected to a fourth term in 1944. Later, in 1951, the Twenty-Second Amendment to the Constitution was adopted, limiting presidential service to two terms.

- Dwight D. Eisenhower was the first President of all fifty states. Hawaii, the fiftieth state, entered the union on August 21, 1959, during Eisenhower's second term.

- Eisenhower was the first President to hold a pilot's license.

- John F. Kennedy, born on May 29, 1917, was the first President born in the twentieth century.

- Lyndon Johnson was the first President to be sworn in by a woman. Johnson took the oath of office on November 22, 1963, following the assassination of John F. Kennedy. The oath was given by Sarah Hughes, a Federal District Judge, in the presidential airplane, at Love Field, Dallas, Texas.

- Richard Nixon was the first President to visit all fifty states.

- Nixon was also the first President to resign (on August 9, 1974).

- Ronald Reagan was the first President to appoint a woman to the Supreme Court. During July 1981, Reagan chose Sandra Day O'Connor to fill a vacancy on the Court.

☆ Birthplaces ☆

The state of Virginia is sometimes referred to as "the Mother of Presidents." That's because Virginia leads all states as the presidential birthplace. Eight Presidents were born in Virginia. Seven Presidents were born in Ohio and four in New York. Here's a state-by-state summary:

Virginia (8)
George Washington
Thomas Jefferson
James Madison
James Monroe
William Henry Harrison
John Tyler
Zachary Taylor
Woodrow Wilson

Ohio (7)
Ulysses S. Grant
Rutherford B. Hayes
James Garfield
Benjamin Harrison
William McKinley
William H. Taft
Warren G. Harding

New York (4)
Martin Van Buren
Millard Fillmore
Theodore Roosevelt
Franklin D. Roosevelt

Massachusetts (3)
John Adams
John Quincy Adams
John F. Kennedy

North Carolina (2)
James K. Polk
Andrew Johnson

Texas (2)
Dwight D. Eisenhower
Lyndon Johnson

Vermont (2)
Chester A. Arthur
Calvin Coolidge

California (1)
Richard M. Nixon

Georgia (1)
Jimmy Carter

Illinois (1)
Ronald Reagan

Iowa (1)
Herbert Hoover

Kentucky (1)
Abraham Lincoln

Missouri (1)
Harry Truman

Nebraska (1)
Gerald Ford

New Hampshire (1)
Franklin Pierce

New Jersey (1)
Grover Cleveland

Pennsylvania (1)
James Buchanan

South Carolina (1)
Andrew Jackson

☆ Presidential Names ☆

Planning on growing up to be President? You have a better chance if your name happens to be James. It's the most common presidential name.

When Jimmy Carter became President in 1977, it marked the sixth time that a James had occupied the White House. Before Carter, there was James

Garfield, James Buchanan, James K. Polk, James Monroe and James Madison.

John is runner-up. There have been four Johns — John Adams, John Quincy Adams, John Tyler and John F. Kennedy.

William takes third place. There have

been three Williams: William Henry Harrison, William McKinley and William Howard Taft.

There have been two Presidents named Franklin — Franklin Pierce and Franklin D. Roosevelt; and two Andrews — Andrew Jackson and Andrew Johnson. All other presidential names have been one of a kind.

Five of the Presidents were not happy with the names they were given at birth, and later changed them. Hiram Ulysses Grant felt uncomfortable with the word his initials spelled. He changed his name to Ulysses Simpson Grant.

Stephen Grover Cleveland dropped his first name and became Grover Cleveland. Thomas Woodrow Wilson and John Calvin Coolidge did the same, becoming Woodrow Wilson and Calvin Coolidge.

David Dwight Eisenhower reversed his first and middle names to become Dwight David Eisenhower.

Seventeen of the thirty-nine Presidents were not given a middle name or even a middle initial. They were George Washington, John Adams, Thomas Jefferson, James Madison, James Monroe,

Andrew Jackson, Martin Van Buren, John Tyler, Zachary Taylor, Millard Fillmore, Franklin Pierce, James Buchanan, Abraham Lincoln, Andrew Johnson, Benjamin Harrison, William McKinley and Theodore Roosevelt.

Harry S. Truman is a special case. The "S" in Harry S. Truman is not an abbreviation for a particular name. It is said to have been chosen to honor his grandparents. Truman's paternal grandfather's name was Shippe (Anderson Shippe Truman). His maternal grandfather's name was Solomon (Solomon Young).

Truman's parents didn't want to show any favoritism toward one grandfather or the other. So they settled the matter through the use of the initial S.

☆ Trivia I ☆

- The engraving of Abraham Lincoln on the $5 bill pictures him in 1864 at the age of 55.

- *Hellcats of the Navy*, a movie produced in 1957, never won an Academy Award. But it has earned lasting fame as the only film in which Ronald Reagan played opposite his wife Nancy.

- When the President travels, the briefcase containing the codes he would need to launch nuclear weapons is carried close to him. The briefcase is called "the football."

- The initials "LBJ" stood for every member of the Johnson family, not just the President, Lyndon Baines Johnson. They stood for Lady Bird Johnson, his wife, and their daughters, Lynda Bird Johnson and Luci Baines Johnson. When the Presi-

dent acquired a small hound with long ears as a pet, he dubbed the pup Little Beagle Johnson.

- During the burial service for Andrew Jackson in June 1845, the President's pet parrot, Poll, had to be removed from the scene for screeching swear words.

- Woodrow Wilson, the twenty-eighth President, typed his own letters.

- By the time he was 57 years old, George Washington was completely toothless.

- Jimmy Carter, a speed reader, was once clocked at 2000 words per minute.

- Thomas Jefferson soaked his feet in cold water every morning to avoid catching colds.

- For two summer vacations while in high school during the early 1930's, Richard Nixon worked as a barker for the wheel-of-chance at the "Slippery Gulch Rodeo" in Prescott, Arizona.

- There have been five bearded Presidents—Abraham Lincoln, Ulysses

S. Grant, Rutherford B. Hayes, James Garfield and Benjamin Harrison. All were Republicans.

- A skilled chef, Dwight Eisenhower was famous for his vegetable soup and charcoal-broiled steaks.

- For exercise, Harry Truman walked two miles every morning at the rapid rate of 128 steps per minute.

- In a poll of historians conducted in 1962, Abraham Lincoln won top ranking as the greatest President of all time.

- At his inauguration on March 4, 1909, William Howard Taft, the heaviest President, weighed 332 pounds.

- The "Baby Ruth" candy bar was named after Grover Cleveland's first daughter, Ruth, born on October 3, 1891. Ruth was five years old when her father was elected President.

- Franklin D. Roosevelt was an avid stamp collector. By the early 1930's, his collection consisted of 40 albums containing more than 25,000 stamps.

- The first telephone was installed in the White House in 1878. Rutherford B. Hayes was President at the time. Hayes's first outgoing call was to Alexander Graham Bell, the inventor of the telephone. The President's first words were: "Please speak more slowly."

- "Death and Destruction" was the name that Grover Cleveland gave to his favorite hunting rifle.
- Calvin Coolidge was the first President to take the oath of office from his father. Coolidge, as Vice President, became President following the death of Warren G. Harding. He was sworn in at the family home in Plymouth, Vermont, at 2:47 A.M. on August 3, 1923. His father, Colonel John Calvin Coolidge, a justice of the peace, administered the oath.

☆ Happy Birthday! ☆

More Presidential birthdays occur in October than any other month. November is runner-up. And no President has ever been born in June. Here's a month-by-month rundown:

January
7, 1800, Millard Fillmore

9, 1913, Richard Nixon

29, 1843, William McKinley

30, 1882, Franklin D. Roosevelt

February

6, 1911, Ronald Reagan

9, 1773, William H. Harrison

12, 1809, Abraham Lincoln

22, 1732, George Washington

March

15, 1767, Andrew Jackson

16, 1751, James Madison

18, 1837, Grover Cleveland

29, 1790, John Tyler

April

13, 1743, Thomas Jefferson

23, 1791, James Buchanan

27, 1822, Ulysses S. Grant

28, 1758, James Monroe

May

8, 1884, Harry S. Truman

29, 1917, John F. Kennedy

June

(None)

July

4, 1872, Calvin Coolidge

11, 1767, John Quincy Adams

14, 1913, Gerald Ford

August

10, 1874, Herbert Hoover

20, 1833, Benjamin Harrison

27, 1908, Lyndon B. Johnson

September

15, 1857, William H. Taft

October

1, 1924, Jimmy Carter

4, 1822, Rutherford B. Hayes

5, 1830, Chester A. Arthur

14, 1890, Dwight D. Eisenhower

27, 1858, Theodore Roosevelt

30, 1735, John Adams

November

2, 1795, James K. Polk

2, 1865, Warren G. Harding

19, 1831, James A. Garfield

23, 1804, Franklin Pierce

24, 1784, Zachary Taylor

December

5, 1782, Martin Van Buren

28, 1856, Woodrow Wilson

29, 1808, Andrew Johnson

☆ Colleges of the Presidents ☆

The parents of Andrew Johnson, the seventeenth President, were too poor to send him to school. He was apprenticed to a tailor at the age of 13.

Fellow workers at the tailor shop taught Andrew the alphabet. He taught himself to read and, when he was 17, his girl friend taught him how to write. By that time, Andrew was running his own tailor shop.

Andrew Johnson was an exception. Most of the Presidents had a formal educational training. Here is a listing of those who graduated from college:

John Adams	Harvard University
Thomas Jefferson	College of William & Mary
James Madison	Princeton University
James Monroe	College of William & Mary
John Quincy Adams	Harvard University
James K. Polk	University of North Carolina
Franklin Pierce	Bowdoin College
James Buchanan	Dickinson College
Ulysses S. Grant	U.S. Military Academy
Rutherford B. Hayes	Kenyon College
James Garfield	Williams College
Chester A. Arthur	Union College
Benjamin Harrison	Miami University (Ohio)

Theodore Roosevelt	Harvard University
William H. Taft	Yale University
Woodrow Wilson	Princeton University
Calvin Coolidge	Amherst College
Herbert Hoover	Stanford University
Franklin D. Roosevelt	Harvard University
Dwight D. Eisenhower	U.S. Military Academy
John F. Kennedy	Harvard University
Lyndon B. Johnson	Southwest Texas State University
Richard Nixon	Whittier College
Gerald Ford	University of Michigan
Jimmy Carter	U.S. Naval Academy
Ronald Reagan	Eureka College

Three Presidents attended college but did not graduate: William H. Harrison (Hampden-Sydney College), William McKinley (Allegheny College) and Warren G. Harding (Ohio Central College).

These Presidents did not attend college:

George Washington	Abraham Lincoln
Andrew Jackson	Andrew Johnson
Martin Van Buren	Grover Cleveland
Zachary Taylor	Harry Truman
Millard Fillmore	

☆ Offspring ☆

Six of the thirty-nine Presidents had no children.

The thirty-three Presidents who did have children had a total of 143 — 85 were boys and 58 were girls.

Here's a rundown:

George Washington (none)

John Adams
3 boys (John Quincy, Charles, Thomas)
2 girls (Abigail, Susanna)

Thomas Jefferson
1 boy (unnamed, died in infancy)
5 girls (Martha Washington, Jane, Mary,
Lucy —died in infancy, Lucy)

James Madison (none)

James Monroe
1 boy (unnamed, died in infancy)
2 girls (Eliza, Maria)

John Quincy Adams
3 boys (George Washington, John Adams,
Charles Francis)
1 girl (Louisa)

Franklin Pierce
3 boys (Franklin, Frank, Benjamin)

James Buchanan (none)

Abraham Lincoln
4 boys (Robert, Edward, William, Thomas)

Andrew Johnson
3 boys (Charles, Robert, Andrew)
2 girls (Martha, Mary)

Ulysses S. Grant
3 boys (Frederick, Ulysses, Jesse)
1 girl (Ellen)

Rutherford B. Hayes
7 boys (Birchard, James, Rutherford, Joseph,
George, Scott, Manning)
1 girl (Fanny)

James Garfield
5 boys (Harry, James, Irvin, Abram, Edward)
2 girls (Eliza, Mary)

Chester A. Arthur
2 boys (William, Chester)
1 girl (Ellen)

Andrew Jackson (none)

Martin Van Buren
4 boys (Abraham, John, Martin, Smith Thompson)

William H. Harrison
6 boys (John Cleves, William, John Scott, Benjamin, Carter, James)
4 girls (Elizabeth, Lucy, Mary, Anna)

John Tyler
By first wife:
3 boys (Robert, John, Tazewell)
5 girls (Mary, Letitia, Elizabeth, Anne, Alice)
By second wife:
5 boys (David, John, Lachlan, Lyon, Robert)
2 girls (Julia, Pearl)

James K. Polk (none)

Zachary Taylor
1 boy (Richard)
5 girls (Anne, Sarah, Octavia, Margaret, Mary)

Millard Fillmore

By first wife:
1 boy (Millard)
1 girl (Mary)
By second wife: (none)

Grover Cleveland

2 boys (Richard, Francis)
3 girls (Ruth, Esther, Marion)

Benjamin Harrison

By first wife:
1 boy (Russell)
1 girl (Mary)
By second wife:
1 girl (Elizabeth)

William McKinley

2 girls (Katherine, Ida)

Theodore Roosevelt

By first wife:
1 girl (Alice)
By second wife:
4 boys (Theodore, Kermit, Archibald,
Quentin)
1 girl (Ethel)

William Howard Taft

2 boys (Robert, Charles)
1 girl (Helen)

Woodrow Wilson

By first wife:
3 girls (Margaret, Jessie, Eleanor)
By second wife: (none)

Warren G. Harding (none)

Calvin Coolidge

2 boys (John, Calvin)

Herbert Hoover

2 boys (Herbert, Jr.; Allan)

Franklin D. Roosevelt

5 boys (James; Franklin Delano, Jr.—died in
infancy; Elliott; Franklin Delano, Jr.; John)
1 girl (Anne)

Harry S. Truman

1 girl (Margaret)

Dwight D. Eisenhower

2 boys (David, John)

John F. Kennedy

2 boys (John, Jr.; Patrick — died in infancy)
1 girl (Caroline)

Lyndon B. Johnson

2 girls (Lynda, Luci)

Richard M. Nixon

2 girls (Patricia, Julie)

Gerald R. Ford

3 boys (Michael, John, Steven)
1 girl (Susan)

James E. Carter

3 boys (Jack, James, Jeffrey)
1 girl (Amy)

Ronald W. Reagan

By first wife:
1 boy (Michael) (adopted)
1 girl (Maureen)
By second wife:
1 boy (Ronald)
1 girl (Patricia)

☆ From the White House Kitchen ☆

One of George Washington's favorite menus included cream of peanut soup, mashed sweet potatoes with coconut, string beans with mushrooms and Martha Washington's whiskey cake.

Thomas Jefferson introduced ice cream, waffles and macaroni to the United States.

Andrew Jackson's favorite dish was turkey hash.

"Soft" gingerbread was one of the most noted dishes to come from the

White House kitchen when Dolley Madison was First Lady. Her recipe included one cup of New Orleans molasses and ⅔ cup of fresh beef drippings.

Although Abraham Lincoln paid little attention to what he ate, he is known to have enjoyed oysters served in a variety of ways and he always had good things to say about his wife's baking.

A favorite breakfast of Ulysses S. Grant was a cucumber soaked in vinegar.

Grover Cleveland loved to dine on corned beef and cabbage.

Economy became the watchword in the White House kitchen when thrifty Calvin Coolidge became President. One chef quit when the President tried to convince him that it would take only six hams to feed sixty people at a state dinner.

Even when dining by themselves, the Herbert Hoovers had seven-course meals.

Mrs. Nesbitt, official housekeeper for the White House during Franklin D. Roosevelt's term in the White House, believed in "plain foods, plainly prepared." Roosevelt quickly became bored with the White House meals. Although he complained, his complaints were never taken seriously. Suggestions he made for more exciting dishes were never followed.

One day in the summer of 1944, Roosevelt was chatting with his daughter Anna and his secretary Grace Tully, when he suddenly said, "You know, I really want to be elected for a fourth term." The two women leaned forward, eager to hear what the President was going to say next. "I want to be elected to a fourth term," said Roosevelt, a grin crossing his face, "so I can fire Mrs. Nesbitt." Roosevelt *was* elected to a fourth term, but Mrs. Nesbitt was never fired.

Dwight D. Eisenhower's favorite dessert was prune whip.

John Kennedy loved fettucini, Italian pasta cut in narrow strips. And for breakfast, Kennedy ordered two eggs, each boiled four minutes.

Lyndon and Lady Bird Johnson brought such Texas specialties as chili, barbecued ribs, corn pudding and pecan pie to the White House.

Richard Nixon often lunched on cottage cheese topped with ketchup.

Gerald Ford's usual breakfast consisted of grapefruit, an English muffin and tea.

☆ White House Pets ☆

When Theodore Roosevelt became President in 1901, the White House suddenly became a very lively place. Roosevelt had six children, and the children loved pets. The Executive Mansion burst at the seams with dogs, cats, squirrels, raccoons, rabbits, guinea pigs, a badger, a black bear, a rat, a parrot and a green garter snake.

The children's favorite pet was a pony named Algonquin. When Archie Roosevelt got the measles and was made to stay in his second floor bedroom, his brothers decided to cheer him up with a visit from Algonquin. How did the Roosevelt boys get Algonquin to the second floor? The way everyone else went up: Algonquin rode in the elevator.

Thomas Jefferson kept a pet mockingbird in his study in the White House. Jefferson taught the bird to ride on his shoulder and take food from his lips.

Zachary Taylor, a hero of the Mexican War of 1846, provided a home for his old war-horse, Whitey, on the White House grounds. But it was not a peaceful existence for poor old Whitey. White House visitors pulled hairs from his tail for souvenirs.

Warren G. Harding kept a pen of turkeys at the White House.

Calvin Coolidge, the thirtieth President, loved animals. Among his many pets was a raccoon named Rebecca that he walked on a leash.

Coolidge also owned a dog named Paul Pry and a cat named Tiger. One

day when Tiger could not be found, the President asked local radio stations to broadcast a "missing cat" bulletin. Tiger was recovered but later ran away again and was never found.

During World War I, (1917–1918), the Woodrow Wilsons, like other American families, did whatever they could to help out. In order to release the White House gardeners for the war effort, the Wilsons kept a flock of sheep on the White House lawn to eat the grass.

The plan worked better than anyone expected. Not only was the grass kept neatly trimmed, but the sheep grew heavy coats of wool. After the sheep were shorn, the wool was sold and the money donated to the Red Cross.

William Howard Taft kept a cow that grazed on the White House lawn. She lived in the garage amidst the President's four automobiles and often supplied the milk that was served in the White House.

Herbert Hoover's son, Allan, had two pet alligators that sometimes were permitted to wander loose around the White House.

The John F. Kennedy family, which

included daughter Caroline and son John, had almost as many pets as the Theodore Roosevelts. The Kennedy menagerie included dogs, a cat, three birds, three ponies, two hamsters and a rabbit.

☆ Mrs. President ☆

The term "First Lady," used to indicate the President's wife, was never applied to Martha Washington. It was not heard, in fact, until 1877, when it was applied to Lucy Hayes, the wife of Rutherford B. Hayes, the nineteenth President.

Here is a collection of First Lady facts:

- Betty Ford sometimes rated higher in the popularity polls than her husband, Gerald. During the 1976 presidential campaign, bumper stickers were sometimes seen that read: VOTE FOR BETTY'S HUSBAND.

- Abigail Adams, First Lady from 1797–1801, brought the first piano to the White House.

- Eleanor Roosevelt, First Lady from 1933–1945, drove her own car and refused Secret Service protection. She agreed, however, to keep a pistol in the glove compartment.

- Lucy Hayes, after becoming First Lady in 1877, would not permit liquor to be served at White House functions. Her stand earned her the nickname "Lemonade Lucy."

- Rainbow was the Secret Service's code name for Nancy Reagan.

- Nancy Reagan isn't the only First Lady to have had an acting career in the movies. During the mid-1930's, when Pat Nixon was attending the University of Southern California, she worked as a Hollywood extra, a person hired for a minor part in a film, such as in a crowd scene.

- Mary Todd Lincoln, the wife of the sixteenth President, has been described as being selfish, spoiled, rude, and arrogant. She once complained so heatedly about food prices to the White House grocer that he quit. President Lincoln called the man into his office, put an arm about his shoulder and said, "Can't you stand for fifteen minutes what I have stood for fifteen years?"

- Abigail Adams, wife of John Adams, the second President, was thought to have much too much influence on her husband. For that, she was sometimes called "Her Majesty."

- Jane Pierce, wife of Franklin Pierce, the fourteenth President, believed

that Washington and politics were evil. When her husband was seeking to be elected in 1852, she prayed that he would lose.

• The Girl Scouts were the pet project of Lou Hoover, wife of the thirty-first President. She once served as the organization's national president.

• Mamie Doud married Dwight D. Eisenhower in 1916, when he was an Army lieutenant. The Eisenhowers had thirty-five homes in thirty-five years at Army posts all over the world.

- Claudia was the baptismal name of Lady Bird Johnson, the wife of Lyndon Johnson, the thirty-sixth President. She was nicknamed by a nursemaid who said she was as "purty as a ladybird."

☆ Good Relations ☆

During 1986, it was reported that Richard Nixon and Jimmy Carter were sixth cousins. Friends of the two found that hard to believe. Carter and Nixon had no comment on the story.

They *are* sixth cousins insisted a Library of Congress genealogist, a specialist in the study of family ancestries. It was explained that Carter and Nixon were both descendants of Robert Morris, an immigrant from Wales who settled in Shrewsbury, New Jersey, long before the American Revolution.

One branch of the family trekked southward, settling in Georgia. That was the Carter branch. Other children went west, where Nixon's great grandmother finally settled.

While the blood relationship of Carter and Nixon may be open to question, a number of other Presidents are known for certain to have been related to one another.

John Adams, the second President, and John Quincy Adams, the sixth President, were father and son. No two Presidents were more closely related than that.

William H. Harrison, the ninth President, was the grandfather of Benjamin Harrison, the twenty-third President.

James Madison, the fourth President, and Zachary Taylor, the twelfth President, were second cousins.

The two Roosevelts were related, too. Franklin D. Roosevelt, the thirty-second President, was the fifth cousin of Theodore Roosevelt, the twenty-sixth President.

☆ On the Money ☆

American Presidents have been honored by countless memorials and monuments, everything from the Gerald R.

Ford Museum in Ann Arbor, Michigan, to John F. Kennedy International Airport in New York. And there's Washington, D.C.; the state of Washington; Jackson, Mississippi; Lincoln, Nebraska, plus hundreds of other cities, towns and counties. In Alaska, an icefield and a towering mountain have been named in the memory of William McKinley.

Our money has also honored the Presidents. Much of our paper money has been adorned with presidential portraits. The gallery includes:

    $1 bill — George Washington
    $2 bill — Thomas Jefferson
    $5 bill — Abraham Lincoln
    $20 bill — Andrew Jackson
    $50 bill — Ulysses S. Grant
   $500 bill — William McKinley
  $1000 bill — Grover Cleveland
  $5000 bill — James Madison

In addition, several non-Presidents appear on U.S. bills. These include: Alexander Hamilton on the $10 bill; Benjamin Franklin on the $100 bill, and Salmon P. Chase, Secretary of the

Treasury from 1861–1864, on the $10,000 bill. (In 1969, the government began withdrawing from circulation bills of $500 and over.)

Six Presidents are depicted on United States coins. Abraham Lincoln was the first President whose portrait appeared on a coin. The design for the Lincoln penny was adopted in April 1909 and coinage began in May that year.

Other presidential coins, along with the date each was first minted include:

George Washington quarter — 1932
Thomas Jefferson nickel — 1938
Franklin Roosevelt dime – 1946
John F. Kennedy half-dollar — 1964
Dwight D. Eisenhower silver dollar — 1971

☆ Professions ☆

Of the thirty-nine Presidents, only one was an actor — Ronald Reagan. One was a tailor — Andrew Johnson. And one was an engineer — Herbert Hoover. Abraham Lincoln and Harry S. Truman were the only storekeepers.

Most of the individuals who became President were lawyers. In fact, twenty-five of the thirty-nine Presidents were practicing attorneys before being elected. They include:

John Adams	James Garfield
Thomas Jefferson	Chester A. Arthur
James Monroe	Grover Cleveland
John Quincy Adams	Benjamin Harrison
Andrew Jackson	William McKinley
Martin Van Buren	Theodore Roosevelt
John Tyler	William H. Taft
James K. Polk	Woodrow Wilson
Millard Fillmore	Calvin Coolidge
Franklin Pierce	Franklin D.
James Buchanan	Roosevelt
Abraham Lincoln	Richard Nixon
Rutherford B. Hayes	Gerald Ford

The next most popular profession was school teaching. Seven Presidents worked as teachers:

John Adams	William McKinley
Millard Fillmore	Warren G. Harding
James Garfield	Lyndon B. Johnson
Chester A. Arthur	

Three Presidents were military men before taking up residence at 1600 Pennsylvania Avenue — Zachary Taylor, Ulysses S. Grant and Dwight D. Eisenhower.

George Washington was, of course, a military leader. Jimmy Carter was a naval officer and Ronald Reagan served with the U.S. Army Air Corps during World War II. But these were not their principal occupations. Washington was a farmer, Carter had a peanut business and Reagan acted in the movies and on TV. Twenty-five of the thirty-nine Presidents saw military service.

☆ Hang in There! ☆

A person who is persistent, says the dictionary, is one who continues to follow the same course of action, no matter what. A persistent person keeps trying and trying.

Abraham Lincoln was persistent. Here's the evidence:

- Lincoln was defeated when he ran for the Illinois House of Representatives in 1832. But he was victorious in the House race in 1834, and was then reelected for three consecutive terms.

- He was defeated when he ran for the U.S. House of Representatives in 1843, then ran successfully for a House seat in 1846.

- He was defeated for the Senate in 1855.

- He was defeated for Vice President in 1856.

- He was defeated for the Senate again in 1858.

- Finally, in 1860, Lincoln was elected President.

☆ Going to the Dogs ☆

When Gerald Ford was President, from 1974–1977, he owned a golden retriever named Liberty. The dog was kept in a kennel on the ground floor of the White House. But when Liberty was about to give birth to a litter, she was moved to a room on the third floor of the White House, to be close to her trainer.

One evening the trainer had to go out. President Ford offered to keep the dog in his bedroom. "Mr. President, she's no trouble at all," said the trainer. "If she wants to go out, she'll come and lick your face."

Sure enough, at about three o'clock the next morning, the President was awakened from a deep sleep when Liberty came lapping. Drowsily, the President put on his robe and slippers, then took the elevator to the ground floor, went outside with Liberty and waited until she returned.

When the President and the dog went back to the house and the President pressed the button for the elevator, nothing happened. Someone had cut

the power. The President and Liberty had no choice but to take the stairs.

At the top of the stairwell was a door that led to the family living quarters. When the President tried to turn the knob, he found the door was locked.

He went back down the stairs to the second floor and tried the door there. It was locked, too. The first floor door was also locked.

Ford got upset. Here he was, the President, and unable to get into the White House. He started pounding on walls. Suddenly, the White House came alive. Lights went on. Doors opened. Secret Service agents appeared. When they found out what had happened, they were embarrassed.

Ford told them not to worry. All he had missed, he said, were a few minutes sleep.

Not long after, Liberty gave birth to nine puppies in the White House. The new mother then went back to living in the White House kennel.

Like Gerald Ford, most Presidents have enjoyed keeping dogs. They're the most popular White House pet by far. The dog-owning Presidents have included Washington, Jefferson, Madison, Monroe, William H. Harrison, Tyler, Taylor, Polk, Jackson, Lincoln, both Roosevelts, Wilson, Harding, Coolidge, Hoover, Nixon, Johnson, Kennedy, Eisenhower, Ford and Reagan.

Franklin D. Roosevelt's Scottie, named Fala, was one of the most famous of all White House dogs. During the summer of 1944, Fala accompanied Roosevelt on a voyage to Hawaii aboard the cruiser *Baltimore*. The President noticed that Fala kept disappearing for hours at a time. In addition, the dog's hair seemed to be falling out in patches.

Upon investigation, the President learned that some of the sailors had been luring Fala to their living quarters by feeding him table scraps. Then the sailors would snip off tufts of Fala's hair for souvenirs. Roosevelt quickly put an end to the feeding and snipping.

During the years of World War II, from 1941 to 1945, when the President traveled by train, his security personnel tried to keep his plans secret. But Fala, who insisted on going for a walk at every train stop, often gave away the fact that the President was passing through town. People who saw and recognized Fala knew that Roosevelt was nearby. The Secret Service agents who guarded the President nicknamed Fala "The Informer."

George Washington bred hounds, treated them like members of the family and gave them unusual names. Among the males were Drunkard, Tarter and Trueman. The females included Duchess, True Love and Sweet Lips.

Warren G. Harding, the twenty-ninth President, owned an Airedale named Laddie Boy who always brought the President his newspapers. When Laddie Boy had a birthday, he was served a cake made of layers of dog biscuits topped with icing.

When President Harding died in office in 1923, the Newsboys Association launched a campaign to have a statue made of Laddie Boy as a tribute to the President. Newsboys throughout the country contributed pennies for the cause. The statue is now on display at the Smithsonian Institution in Washington, D.C.

Herbert Hoover once issued an order

forbidding members of his White House staff to pet his dog, King Tut. The problem was that King Tut was getting so much love and affection from everyone else that he was ignoring the President.

Lyndon B. Johnson, in his seven years in the White House (1963–1969), owned several dogs. One of them, Yuki, was provided with plastic boots to wear when it rained.

Edgar was a gift from J. Edgar Hoover, the director of the Federal Bureau of Investigation. When Edgar arrived, Bianca, another Johnson dog, became jealous of the newcomer and bit Edgar so severely that several stitches were required.

Johnson's best known dogs were a pair of beagles, Him and Her. On January 20, 1965, Him won lasting fame when Johnson brought the dog to his inaugural parade. No other White House pet had ever been so honored.

When Him was issued Washington, D.C., dog license No. 1 and Her received license No. 2, it triggered a controversy. Did this mean, a reporter wanted to know, that the President had abandoned his pledge to give women equal opportunity?

Johnson got into real trouble when he was once photographed lifting Him by the ears. When the photo appeared in newspapers throughout the country, angry dog lovers by the thousands wrote or telephoned the White House to protest.

Late in 1985, President and Mrs. Reagan were presented with a nine-week-old sheepdog. Tiny and cuddly, the puppy was named Lucky.

Lucky grew fast. Within months, she stood more than two feet tall and weighed around eighty pounds. "She's like a little pony," said a member of the First Lady's staff.

Mrs. Reagan had a hard time controlling Lucky whenever she tried to walk the dog on a leash. "At times it looks like Mrs. Reagan is water skiing or skateboarding behind the dog," said another White House staff member. "There's a real fear she's going to fall down."

Lucky was given five weeks of obedience training but unfortunately it didn't help. She still had too much energy.

The final solution was to send Lucky to the Reagans' California ranch, where she would have four other dogs for company and wide open spaces to run in.

Lucky was replaced at the White House by Rex, a year-old King Charles spaniel — not as much fun as Lucky but better behaved. Nancy Reagan could take Rex for a walk without becoming involved in a tug-of-war.

☆ Trivia II ☆

- James Buchanan, who served from 1857–1861, is said to have had the neatest handwriting of any President.

- August 27, the birthdate of Lyndon B. Johnson, is a legal holiday in Texas. Johnson was born near Stonewall, Texas, in 1908.

- Proper White House etiquette demands that the President be served first at meals. No one is allowed to leave the table before the President. When he enters a room, everyone who is seated must rise.

- William McKinley, the twenty-fifth President, loved to smoke cigars. But he would not permit himself to be photographed with one. He said he did not want to set a bad example for the children of America.

- Thomas Jefferson was the inventor of the swivel chair.

- Abraham Lincoln's favorite pastime was said to be swapping stories with friends.

- Richard Nixon, when he ran for a second term in 1972, was the first President for whom 18-year-olds could vote. The Twenty-Sixth Amendment to the Constitution, which reduced the voting age from 21 to 18, was adopted in 1971.

- Three American Presidents were left-handed: James Garfield, Harry Truman and Gerald Ford.

- Calvin Coolidge is the only President to have been born on the Fourth of July (July 4, 1872).

- Dwight D. Eisenhower introduced helicopters to the White House for short trips.

- In 1890, during the administration of Benjamin Harrison, electric lights were installed in the White House, replacing gas lights and candles. The Harrisons, like many people of the day, were a bit fearful of electricity. They would never turn the lights on or off by themselves but always instructed the servants to do so.

- James Buchanan is the only President who never married.

☆ Wit and Wisdom ☆

While most of the Presidents were not noted for their wit or humor, some of them said things that were funny to the people of their times and still bring a smile today. Here are some examples:

One day a friend was visiting Theodore Roosevelt in the White House. Roosevelt's young daughter Alice kept popping in and out of the office and interrupting them.

"Theodore," the friend finally complained, "Isn't there something you can do to control Alice?"

Roosevelt answered firmly: "I can do one of two things. I can be President of the United States or I can control Alice. I cannot do both."

Abraham Lincoln sometimes made jokes about his homely looks. When Senator Stephen A. Douglas called him a "two-faced man," Lincoln replied, "If I had another face, do you think I would wear this one?"

Music appreciation was not a subject in which Ulysses S. Grant could ever expect high marks. He was tone deaf. "I only know two tunes," he once said. "One of them is 'Yankee Doodle' and the other isn't."

Calvin Coolidge, the thirtieth President, never wasted words. His nickname was "Silent Cal."

A reporter once said to him: "I bet someone that I could get more than two words out of you."

Replied Cal: "You lose."

A messenger from the Treasury Department delivered Coolidge's first paycheck as President. As the boy was departing, Coolidge said to him, "Call again."

"When I hear anyone arguing for slavery," Abraham Lincoln once said, "I feel a strong impulse to see it tried on him personally."

Franklin D. Roosevelt, the thirty-second President, once gave this advice to his son James on how to make a successful speech: "Be sincere, be brief, be seated."

In the spring of 1961, not long after he had been inaugurated, John F. Kennedy met with Soviet Premier Nikita Khrushchev in Vienna. During one of their conferences, Kennedy noticed a medal on Khrushchev's chest and asked him what it was. Khrushchev replied that it was the Lenin Peace Prize. "I hope you keep it," Kennedy said.

After reading an article that praised him in glowing terms, President Lyndon B. Johnson turned to a member of his staff and said: "I wish my mother and father could read this. My father would enjoy it. My mother would believe it."

When the newly decorated White House Press Room was being dedicated,

Ronald Reagan reminded reporters that the room was built over what had once been a swimming pool. Then he added, "It isn't true, however, that the floor is hinged and can be sprung like a trap."

Harry Truman's father, John Anderson Truman, a farmer and livestock dealer, was judged by many to be a failure. Truman protested. "My father was not a failure," he said. "After all, he was the father of the President of the United States."

☆ TV Pioneers ☆

Scarcely a day passes that the President doesn't appear on television. He is, in fact, as much a fixture on home screens as Bill Cosby or soft-drink commercials.

This tradition is almost fifty years old. It dates back to April 30, 1939, when President Franklin D. Roosevelt made a trip to New York for the opening of the World's Fair.

Television was in its infancy then. The Radio Corporation of America, the parent company of NBC at the time,

had sent its first experimental signals from the tower of the Empire State Building in 1935. The following year, the company installed television receivers in 150 homes in the New York area.

When the World's Fair opened in 1939, NBC decided to be there with its cameras. Roosevelt's speech, delivered from the Federal Building at the Fair, was one of the events covered.

The United States entered World War II in 1941, and television broadcasting was suspended until after the war ended in 1945.

On April 12, 1945, Harry Truman, Vice President at the time, succeeded to the presidency following Roosevelt's death. Truman was the first President to be televised from the White House. On October 5, 1947, a speech of Truman's about the world food crisis was carried by stations in New York City; Schenectady, New York; and Philadelphia.

Dwight D. Eisenhower was the first President to have a news conference covered by television. The date was January 19, 1955.

Several months later, Eisenhower became the first President whose image was telecast in color. Ike was filmed on June 6, 1955, as he addressed a reunion of the class of 1915 of the U.S. Military Academy at West Point, New York.

The film was shown on "The Home Show" on NBC-TV the next day, June 7, 1955.

☆ Nicknames ☆

Once, when Dwight D. Eisenhower was President, a White House visitor asked his young grandson, David, what his name was.

"Dwight David Eisenhower," the boy replied.

Then, said the visitor, pointing to the President who was seated nearby, "Who is he?"

David grinned. "That's Ike," he said.

It's true. To the newspapers of the time, to his friends and to the public, Dwight D. Eisenhower was known as Ike.

It's traditional for the President to be given a nickname or two. Some, like Eisenhower's, make the owner seem a friend. Other names call attention to an outstanding personal quality or stress some accomplishment. Still others are meant to mock the owner.

Here are some examples:

George Washington
Father of His Country
Sage of Mount Vernon
The Surveyor President

Thomas Jefferson
Father of the Declaration of Independence
Sage of Monticello

James Madison
Father of the Constitution
Jemmy

Andrew Jackson
Hero of New Orleans
King Andrew the First
Old Hickory
The People's President

Zachary Taylor
Old Rough and Ready

Abraham Lincoln
The Great Emancipator
Honest Abe
The Martyr President

Ulysses S. Grant
Hero of Appomattox

Grover Cleveland
Uncle Jumbo

Theodore Roosevelt
The Great White Chief
The Hero of San Juan Hill
Rough Rider
Teddy
TR

Woodrow Wilson
Professor

Calvin Coolidge
Silent Cal

Dwight D. Eisenhower
General Ike
Ike

John F. Kennedy
JFK

Lyndon B. Johnson
LBJ
Landslide Lyndon

Gerald R. Ford
Jerry
Mr. Nice Guy

James E. Carter
Jimmy

Ronald Reagan
Dutch
Ron
Ronnie

☆ Good Sports ☆

During his college years at Eureka College in Illinois, Ronald Reagan was a member of the track team and he also played football. "He was a plugger," his coach once said of him. "He was not a star but he was dedicated and worked very hard." Reagan was a lineman; he played guard.

Reagan was also a powerful swimmer. During summer vacations, he worked as a lifeguard at Lowell Park, a recreation area on the Rock River in Dixon, Illinois, where the Reagan family lived.

Reagan is said to have put a notch in a log every time he saved a person from drowning. In seven summers as a lifeguard, he made seventy-seven notches.

Most American Presidents have shown a healthy interest in sports. Partly, no doubt, because it is smart politics to do so. While some have merely watched sports, about half of the Presidents have been physically vigorous men who, like Ronald Reagan, enjoyed participating.

The favorite sports of the Presidents

have been riding, fishing and swimming. George Washington, Thomas Jefferson, Andrew Jackson, Martin Van Buren, Zachary Taylor, Ulysses S. Grant, William McKinley, Theodore Roosevelt, William Howard Taft, Woodrow Wilson, Warren G. Harding, Lyndon B. Johnson and Ronald Reagan were all excellent horsemen.

Ulysses S. Grant could break wild ponies, jump thoroughbreds and even perform acrobatic feats on horseback. While at the Military Academy at West Point in the early 1840's, Grant was only a fair student. But he was the best horseman in his class. "It was as good as a circus to see Grant ride," a classmate of his once said.

When Grant became President in 1869, he ordered the White House stables to be rebuilt. He added horses so that he had more than a dozen from which to choose.

Grant was once arrested in Washington for speeding in his horse and carriage. When the arresting officer recognized Grant, he was ready to let the President go. But Grant insisted that the man do his job and write out a summons. Later Grant commended him.

Thomas Jefferson, John Quincy Adams, William McKinley, Franklin D. Roosevelt and John F. Kennedy were among the Presidents who were skilled swimmers.

Adams enjoyed rising before dawn to slip down to the Potomac River for a swim in the nude. He would leave his clothes on the riverbank. One morning someone stole his clothes while he was in the water. Adams had to send a passing boy running to the White House to get replacements.

Adams also enjoyed the game of billiards and ordered a billiard table for the White House. The public objected to what was branded a foolish purchase. Adams, to quiet the criticism, paid for the table out of his own pocket.

Abraham Lincoln, who stood six feet four and weighed 180 pounds, won wide acclaim as a wrestler early in his life. He scored his first important victory over a street brawler named Jack Armstrong. The bout took place during the period Lincoln was working as a clerk in New Salem, Illinois. The match was arranged when a local saloon-keeper offered Lincoln ten dollars if he could throw Armstrong.

People came from as far away as fifty miles to see the match, and there was a great deal of betting. Armstrong, shorter than Lincoln but powerfully built, was favored. But once the bout began, it was no contest. "Lincoln lifted him by the throat," wrote Carl Sandburg, the President's biographer, "shook him like a rag and then slammed him to a hard fall." The defeated Armstrong could only shake his head in bewilderment.

Grover Cleveland loved hunting and fishing. He was, in fact, often criticized by the newspapers of his time for the long trips he took in quest of fish or game.

Cleveland was not satisfied to fish for just a couple of hours. His fishing trips lasted for days. A good catch of fish might number into the hundreds.

Calvin Coolidge, who took office in 1923, also enjoyed fishing. But he went about it daintily. He always wore gloves. Bait was put on the hook for him. Any fish that Coolidge caught was then removed from the hook. The Secret

Service men assigned to guard Coolidge complained bitterly when they were asked to perform these duties, which they did not consider part of their job of protecting the President.

Coolidge also found relaxation in pitching hay. Rutherford B. Hayes, the nineteenth President, liked to play croquet. Franklin D. Roosevelt and John F. Kennedy both enjoyed sailing.

Theodore Roosevelt, the twenty-sixth President, who held office from 1901–1909, took part in a wide range of sports. As a boy, Roosevelt was thin and sickly. When he was 10 years old, his father took him aside and said to him, "Theodore, you have the mind but you do not have the body. You must *make* your body."

Young Theodore began working out in a gym that his father installed for him on the second floor of their home in New York City. He took boxing lessons, studied judo, learned to ride and shoot, played tennis, took long hikes, hunted big game in Africa and explored the rain forests of Brazil.

During the period of his presidency, 1901–1909, Roosevelt would take part

in exercise at almost any time at any place. His urge to keep trim and fit led to the formation of the "tennis cabinet," a group of cabinet members and friends from Congress and the diplomatic corps who shared the President's enthusiasm for physical fitness.

While Roosevelt saw value in physical exercise, he was not a fanatic about sports. He was the first President to campaign for reforms in certain sports to make them less dangerous. His chief target was college football, a violent game in the early 1900's and one that frequently produced serious injuries and even some deaths. Roosevelt's interest in cleaning up the game led to changes in the rules that helped to make football much safer.

Woodrow Wilson, President from 1913–1921, was an ardent golfer, although handicapped by poor eyesight. "My right eye is like a horse's," he once said. "I can see straight out of it but not sideways. As a result, I cannot take a full swing because my nose gets in the way and cuts off my view of the ball."

Despite his limitations, Wilson played golf every day before breakfast. When the White House lawn was covered with snow and Wilson's practice sessions were threatened, he ordered the balls painted black so they would be seen in the snow.

Dwight D. Eisenhower, who occupied the White House from 1953–1961, is also remembered as a dedicated golfer. As in Wilson's case, Eisenhower's critics thought he devoted too much time to the game and not enough to the presidency.

One day a visitor to the White House

noticed that Eisenhower was wearing a leather bandage on his left wrist. The President explained he had a touch of arthritis. The visitor said he was glad it wasn't serious. "I should say it *is* serious," Eisenhower exclaimed. "It means I can't play golf!"

Eisenhower had a putting green built just outside the Oval Office. Ducking out to tune up his stroke enabled him to relax.

As a boy, Eisenhower was a gifted athlete. At the U.S. Military Academy at West Point, where he had only a fair academic record, he played left halfback on the football team. His career came to an end, however, when he seriously damaged his knee attempting to tackle the great Jim Thorpe.

John F. Kennedy also had his career as an amateur athlete halted by a football injury. Kennedy's involved his back and occurred when he was a student at Harvard. During World War II, when he served in the Navy, Kennedy's back problems got worse. Nevertheless, after he became President, he occasionally played touch football with family members and close friends. Some well-publicized games were played on the White House lawn.

☆ Trivia III ☆

• Lyndon B. Johnson, as an 8-year-old, got six A's and one C+ on his report card. The A's were for arithmetic, geography, grammar, spelling, reading and writing. The C+ was for conduct.

- In 1846, at the age of 79, John Quincy Adams took his last nude dip in the Potomac River.

- John Quincy Adams, who served from 1825–1829, is the first President of whom a photograph exists.

- The only foreign country with a capital named for an American President is Liberia. The capital is Monrovia, which is named in honor of James Monroe, the fifth President.

- Andrew Jackson loved to chew tobacco. When he moved into the White House in 1829, he ordered spittoons for the parlors.

- Ulysses S. Grant smoked twenty cigars a day.

- To the U.S. Postal Service, the White House is 1600 Pennsylvania Avenue. But to the National Park Service, part of the Department of the Interior, it is Reservation No. 1 of the National Capital Parks.

- Grover Cleveland was the twenty-second President. He was also the twenty-fourth President. He is the only President to serve two nonconsecutive terms.

- Warren G. Harding, elected in 1921, was the first President for whom women could cast their ballots. The Nineteenth Amendment to the Constitution, adopted in 1920, granted women the right to vote.

- When Millard Fillmore became President in 1850, he ordered a cast-iron stove for the White House kitchen. Until Fillmore's purchase, all cooking had been done over open fireplaces.

- Thomas Jefferson imported plants for study. He was the first President to grow a tomato. He was, in fact, the first person in America to grow a tomato. At the time, people thought tomatoes were poisonous.

- Four state capitals have been named after Presidents: Jackson, Mississippi; Jefferson City, Missouri; Lincoln, Nebraska; and Madison, Wisconsin.

☆ White House Curse ☆

Beginning in 1840 and extending for well over a century, every President elected in a year ending in a zero died in office. This strange twist of fate was called the "20-year curse" because it occurred every twenty years. Consider:

• William Henry Harrison, elected in 1840.

Harrison caught a cold at his inauguration and died of pneumonia a month later.

• Abraham Lincoln, elected in 1860, and reelected four years later.

Lincoln was assassinated on April 14, 1865.

• James A. Garfield, elected in 1880.

Garfield was shot on July 2, 1881, and three months later died of blood poisoning.

• William McKinley, elected in 1900.

McKinley was shot on September 6, 1901, and died a week later.

• Warren G. Harding, elected in 1920.

Harding died of a heart attack

approximately 2½ years after taking office.

- Franklin D. Roosevelt, elected in 1940 for a third term.

  Roosevelt died of natural causes on April 12, 1945, less than four months after taking the oath of office for a fourth term.

- John F. Kennedy, elected in 1960.

  Kennedy was assassinated on November 22, 1963.

Ronald Reagan, elected in 1980, loomed as the next victim of the curse. About two months after taking office, Reagan was shot and wounded by John F. Hinckley. But quick and expert medical attention saved the President's life. Reagan's survival was said to have broken the curse.

☆A Presidential Curiosity ☆

How does one explain the many similarities in the lives of Abraham Lincoln and John F. Kennedy? Consider:

- Both were married in their thirties to women in their twenties.

- Lincoln won election to the U.S. House of Representatives in 1846. Kennedy was elected to the House in 1946.

- Lincoln tried and failed to get his party's nomination for Vice President in 1856. Kennedy failed in his bid to get his party's nomination for Vice President in 1956.

- Lincoln was elected President in 1860, defeating Stephen A. Douglas, born in 1813. Kennedy was elected President in 1960, defeating Richard Nixon, born in 1913.

- Lincoln was younger than his Vice President, Andrew Johnson, a Southerner, born in 1808. Kennedy was younger than his Vice President, Lyndon B. Johnson, a Southerner, born in 1908.

- Lincoln was shot on a Friday (April 14, 1865) as he sat next to his wife. Kennedy was shot on a Friday (November 22, 1963) as he sat next to his wife.

- Lincoln's assassin, John Wilkes Booth, fled and was killed before he could be brought to trial. Kennedy's assassin, Lee Harvey Oswald, fled and was killed before he could be brought to trial.

☆ Take Me Out to the Ball Game ☆

On April 7, 1986, a sunny Monday, President Ronald Reagan traveled from Washington about fifty miles north and east to Memorial Stadium in Baltimore to throw out the opening pitch of the 1986 baseball season. As he took his seat in the presidential box, the record crowd welcomed him with a standing ovation and chants of "Ronnie."

Reagan's first throw to Baltimore catcher Rick Dempsey was high and wide. Dempsey couldn't even get a glove on it. But Reagan's next pitch was down the middle.

This was Reagan's third visit to Memorial Stadium for the opening game of the baseball season. In throwing out the season's first ball, President Reagan was following a custom that had been established in 1910. President William

Howard Taft occupied the White House at the time.

The date was April 10. The scene was Griffith Stadium. The hometown Washington Senators faced the Philadelphia Athletics. Taft, who hailed baseball as "a clean, straight game," loved the experience. The Senators won, 3–0, with the President staying at the park until the final out.

Taft established a tradition. In the decades that followed, Woodrow Wilson, Warren G. Harding, Calvin Coolidge, Herbert Hoover and Franklin D. Roosevelt all lent the dignity of the office of the President to baseball's opening day.

Harry S. Truman, who followed Roosevelt in office, serving from 1945–1953, also loved the opportunity of tossing out the first ball. It gave Truman a chance to show off. Since he was ambidextrous, he could throw the ball using either his left or right hand.

Dwight D. Eisenhower, Truman's successor in the White House, had once been an outfielder for the U.S. Military Academy—and it showed. Long-time observers of the Presidential throw

claimed that Eisenhower displayed a pitching form superior to that of any of his predecessors.

But Eisenhower's talent was overshadowed by that of John F. Kennedy. On April 10, 1961, Kennedy stood up in his box seat at Robert F. Kennedy Stadium in Washington and rifled a sky-high throw that sailed over the heads of almost all the assembled players. Jim Rivera, an outfielder for the Chicago White Sox, who happened to be playing deep deep, gloved the ball. "He can really fire that ball," noted Al Lopez, manager of the White Sox.

Lyndon B. Johnson followed Kennedy in the role and Richard Nixon was next. Nixon was the eleventh President to throw out the first ball at a baseball opener in Washington.

By Nixon's time, Presidents had attended openers in Washington on 46 occasions. Vice Presidents had substituted ten times and other dignitaries had filled in on five occasions.

The tradition was threatened in 1971. That year the curtain came down on major league baseball in the nation's capital. The Senators moved to Arlington, Texas, and became the Texas Rangers.

With the Senators gone from Washington, nobody seemed to care about the first throw any more. The tradition seemed to belong to American history. One exception was an opening-season toss by Richard Nixon at Anaheim Stadium in Orange County, California, in April 1973.

Presidents Ford and Carter, who followed Nixon in the White House, steered clear of the opening game ceremony. Carter made no secret of the fact that he preferred playing softball to watching baseball.

Ronald Reagan revived the tradition in 1984, journeying to Memorial Stadium in Baltimore for the ceremony. Now the city of Washington is campaigning to get a major league franchise to replace the team that departed in 1971. If that happens, the first-ball tradition is almost certain to resume on a regular basis.

☆ Getting in Touch ☆

"How many pets live in the White House?"

"What are your hobbies?"

"Is it possible to obtain a flag that has flown over the White House?"

These are some of the questions frequently asked by boys and girls when writing to the President, according to a White House spokesperson.

Do you have a question that you

would like to ask the President or First Lady? It's easy to do. Simply write a letter.

Use this address:

    The White House
    1600 Pennsylvania Ave.
    Washington, DC 20500

As a salutation, use Dear Sir or Dear Mr. President.

In the case of the First Lady, it's Dear Mrs. (last name).

It's not very likely that you'll get a personal letter from the President or First Lady in return. Mail for the White House arrives by the bagful almost every day. It's not possible for the President or First Lady to respond individually to each letter. But your letter will be answered.

During 1986, anywhere from 2000 to 4000 letters arrived each week just from children. "We try to answer every one," said a White House staff member. "Volunteers do the reading. We usually reply with a booklet or newsletter that serves to answer the question asked."

In reply to a current events question, the letter-writer was likely to receive an eight-page illustrated newsletter that explained the President's position on several different topics. Recent newsletters discussed "Prayer in School," "The Young Astronaut Program," "Central America" and "Financial Aid for College Students."

Boys and girls who asked personal questions — "How much salary do you get?" "What is your favorite song?" — received a handsome 28-page booklet with color photos titled "The President's

House." It contained historical information about the White House and biographical notes about its residents.

Each week, the President is given a sampling of the letters received from children. Sometimes he replies personally to these letters.

If you're hoping for a personal reply from the President, put some thought into your letter. "Ask something original," says Herman Darvick, president of the Universal Autograph Collectors Club. "Ask a question that can be answered only by the President himself, not by an assistant or a secretary."

The Presidents ✯ Years Served

	President	Years Served
1.	George Washington	1789–1797
2.	John Adams	1797–1801
3.	Thomas Jefferson	1801–1809
4.	James Madison	1809–1817
5.	James Monroe	1817–1825
6.	John Quincy Adams	1825–1829
7.	Andrew Jackson	1829–1837
8.	Martin Van Buren	1837–1841
9.	William Henry Harrison	1841
10.	John Tyler	1841–1845
11.	James Knox Polk	1845–1849
12.	Zachary Taylor	1849–1850
13.	Millard Fillmore	1850–1853
14.	Franklin Pierce	1853–1857
15.	James Buchanan	1857–1861
16.	Abraham Lincoln	1861–1865
17.	Andrew Johnson	1865–1869
18.	Ulysses Simpson Grant	1869–1877
19.	Rutherford Birchard Hayes	1877–1881
20.	James Abram Garfield	1881
21.	Chester Alan Arthur	1881–1885
22.	Grover Cleveland	1885–1889
23.	Benjamin Harrison	1889–1893
24.	Grover Cleveland	1893–1897
25.	William McKinley	1897–1901
26.	Theodore Roosevelt	1901–1909

27.	William Howard Taft	1909–1913
28.	Woodrow Wilson	1913–1921
29.	Warren Gamaliel Harding	1921–1923
30.	Calvin Coolidge	1923–1929
31.	Herbert Clark Hoover	1929–1933
32.	Franklin Delano Roosevelt	1933–1945
33.	Harry S. Truman	1945–1953
34.	Dwight David Eisenhower	1953–1961
35.	John Fitzgerald Kennedy	1961–1963
36.	Lyndon Baines Johnson	1963–1969
37.	Richard Milhous Nixon	1969–1974
38.	Gerald R. Ford	1974–1977
39.	James E. Carter, Jr.	1977–1981
40.	Ronald W. Reagan	1981–1988